Draw people in the windows of the taxi and subway train.

New York City, known affectionately as The Big Apple, is a very busy place but traveling around is easy. You can ride on a bus, take a train, or drive around in a taxi. You can also rent a bike or take a boat trip around the harbor. How did you travel around the city?

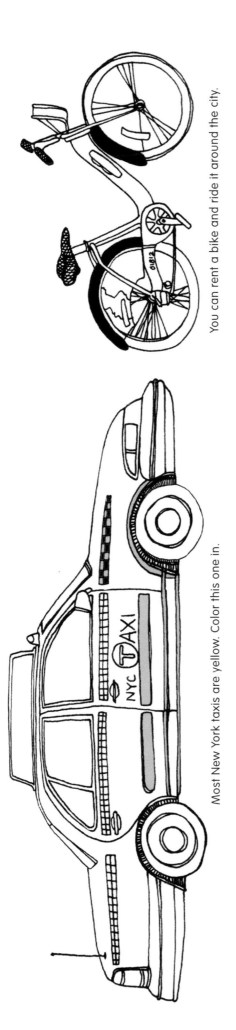

Most New York taxis are yellow. Color this one in.

You can rent a bike and ride it around the city.

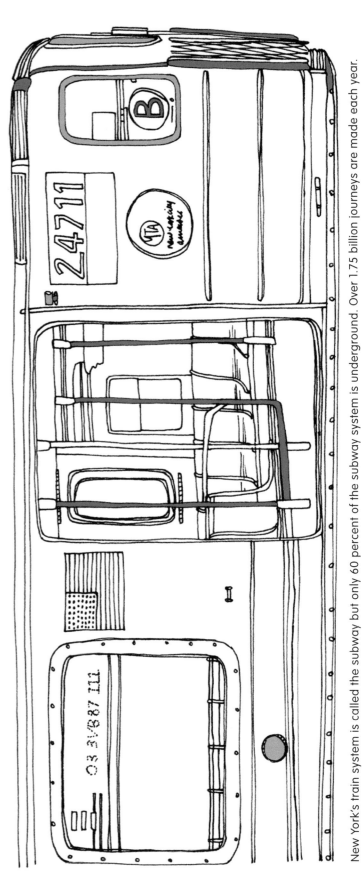

New York's train system is called the subway but only 60 percent of the subway system is underground. Over 1.75 billion journeys are made each year.

Draw some different ways you think people will travel around New York in the future.

Completed in 1931, the quarter-mile-high (0.4km) Empire State Building was the tallest building in New York until 1970. The top floors have different colored lights that honor different occasions—red for Valentine's day, red, white, and blue for Independence Day. Take the elevator to the Observation Deck on the 86th floor for a bird's-eye view of Manhattan. From the 102nd floor, on a clear day you can see up to 80 miles (125km) and five different states.

Draw the other half of the Empire State Building.

Every year, there is a race up to the 86th floor, which means running up 1,576 steps! The current record for the fastest time is 9 minutes and 33 seconds. How far do you think you could run in this time?

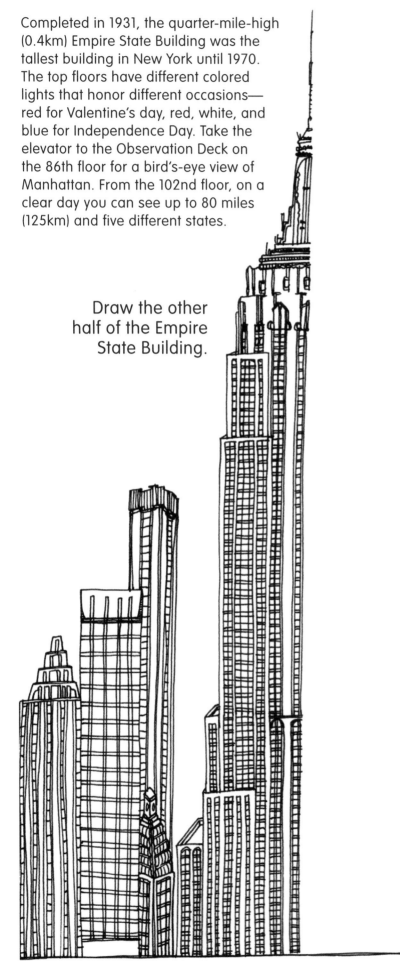

The Empire State Building has featured in over 250 movies! Its most famous role was in the 1933 film *King Kong*, when a giant ape climbed to the top. Draw a picture of King Kong, or another big animal, on top of the Empire State Building.

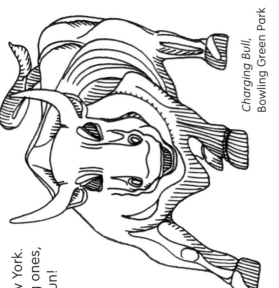

Charging Bull,
Bowling Green Park

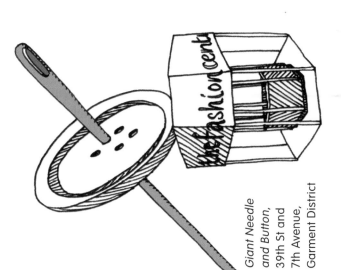

There are lots of statues and sculptures in New York. Look around and you will see many interesting ones, from a giant needle and button to a knotted gun! Which is your favorite?

Draw your own statue on the plinth below. Where would you put it in the city—in a park or outside a building?

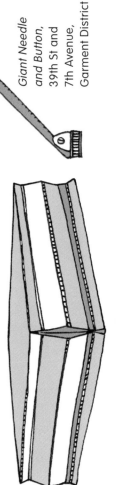

Giant Needle and Button, 39th St and 7th Avenue, Garment District

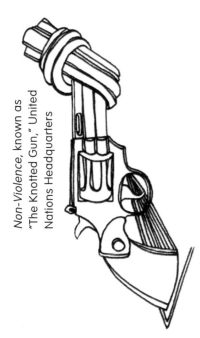

Non-Violence, known as "The Knotted Gun," United Nations Headquarters

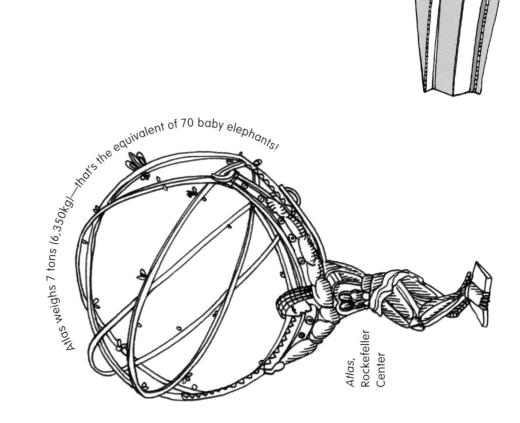

Atlas weighs 7 tons (6,350kg)—that's the equivalent of 70 baby elephants!

Atlas, Rockefeller Center

Draw some more statues you have seen in New York.

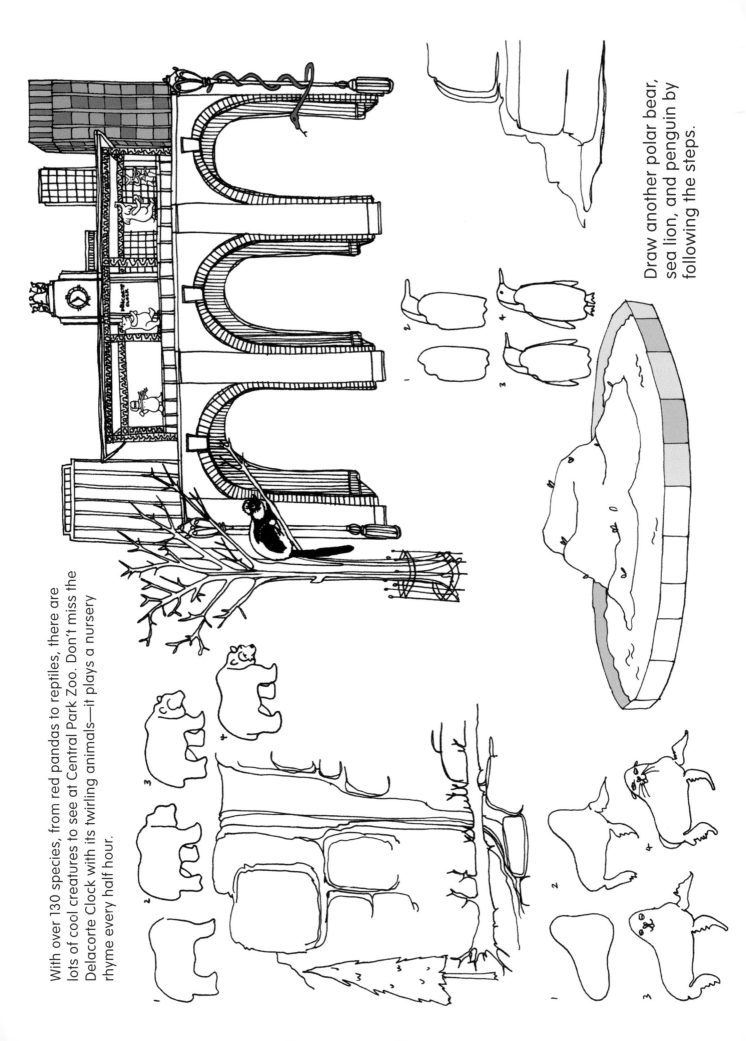

With over 130 species, from red pandas to reptiles, there are lots of cool creatures to see at Central Park Zoo. Don't miss the Delacorte Clock with its twirling animals—it plays a nursery rhyme every half hour.

Draw another polar bear, sea lion, and penguin by following the steps.

Put a tick by them if you saw these animals:

sea lion
lemur
snow leopard
red panda
grizzly bear
tufted puffin

Draw your favorite animals.

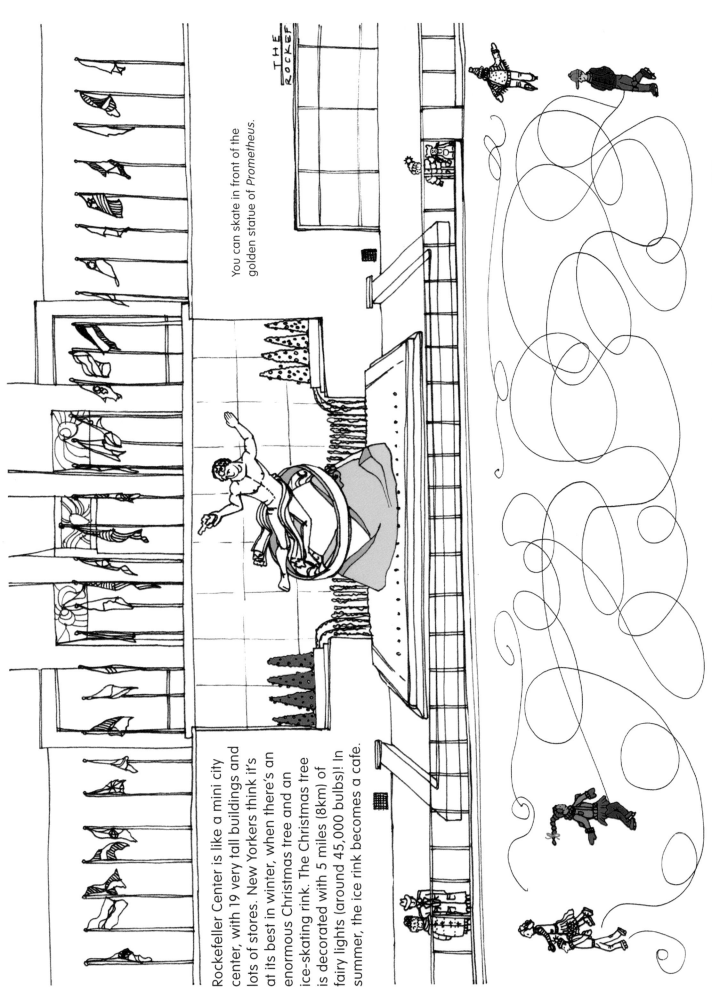

Rockefeller Center is like a mini city center, with 19 very tall buildings and lots of stores. New Yorkers think it's at its best in winter, when there's an enormous Christmas tree and an ice-skating rink. The Christmas tree is decorated with 5 miles (8km) of fairy lights (around 45,000 bulbs)! In summer, the ice rink becomes a cafe.

You can skate in front of the golden statue of *Prometheus*.

Get the ice skater to her partner by following the lines. Try to do it without taking your pen off the page!

Rockefeller Center is famous for its huge tree at Christmas.
Draw a Christmas tree and a picture of you ice skating beneath it.

Broadway, or the "Great White Way" (it got its name from all the lightbulbs), is New York's theater district. There are 40 theaters around here. Have you been to see a show?

Draw a scene and the actors from your favorite show.

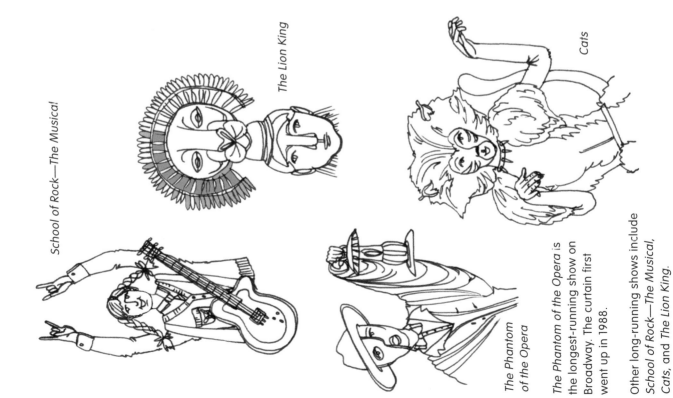

School of Rock—The Musical

The Lion King

Cats

The Phantom of the Opera

The Phantom of the Opera is the longest-running show on Broadway. The curtain first went up in 1988.

Other long-running shows include School of Rock—The Musical, Cats, and The Lion King.

Design a poster to advertise your favorite show.

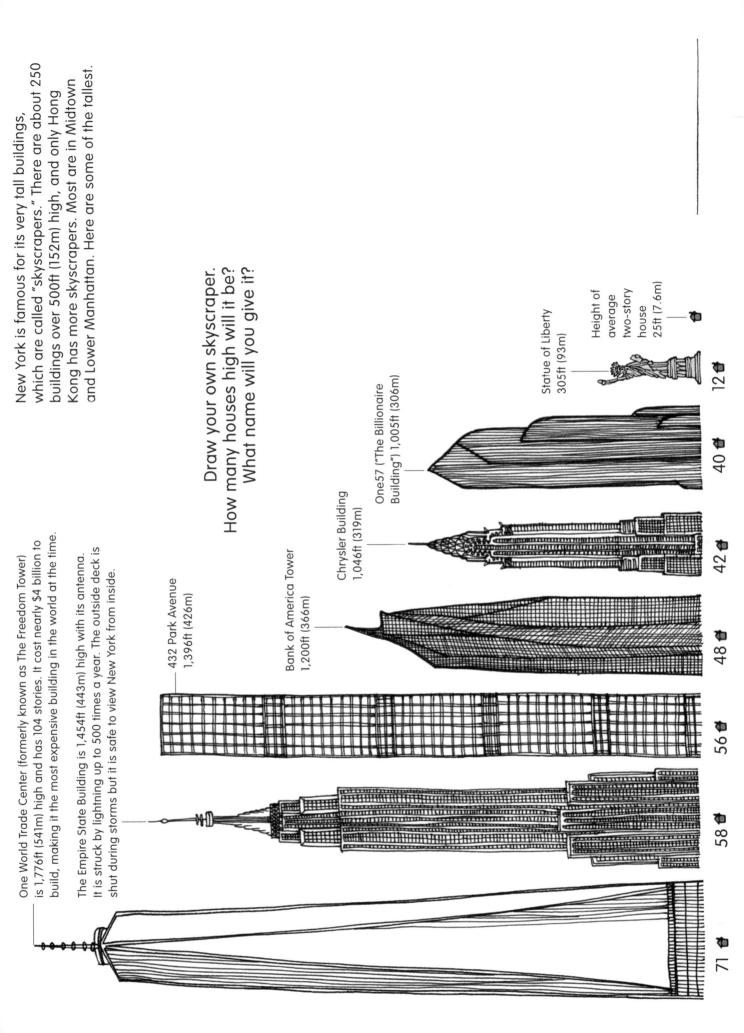

New York is famous for its very tall buildings, which are called "skyscrapers." There are about 250 buildings over 500ft (152m) high, and only Hong Kong has more skyscrapers. Most are in Midtown and Lower Manhattan. Here are some of the tallest.

One World Trade Center (formerly known as The Freedom Tower) is 1,776ft (541m) high and has 104 stories. It cost nearly $4 billion to build, making it the most expensive building in the world at the time.

The Empire State Building is 1,454ft (443m) high with its antenna. It is struck by lightning up to 500 times a year. The outside deck is shut during storms but it is safe to view New York from inside.

Draw your own skyscraper.
How many houses high will it be?
What name will you give it?

432 Park Avenue
1,396ft (426m)

Bank of America Tower
1,200ft (366m)

Chrysler Building
1,046ft (319m)

One57 ("The Billionaire Building") 1,005ft (306m)

Statue of Liberty
305ft (93m)

Height of average two-story house
25ft (7.6m)

71 🏠   58 🏠   56 🏠   48 🏠   42 🏠   40 🏠   12 🏠

Draw a tall building you have seen on your visit to New York.
How many houses high do you think it is? Do you know its name?

Central Park is where New York's children come to play and so can you! Go for a walk, watch a show, ride a carousel horse, go skating, listen to a story, or watch miniature sailboat races.

Central Park has featured in over 300 movies, including *Stuart Little*, *Elf*, and *Enchanted*.

Can you see 6 birds in the picture?

Can you spot 5 differences between the rowers?

Find the *Alice in Wonderland* sculpture and pretend you're at the Mad Hatter's tea party.

Draw a picture of you and a friend sitting in the carriage.

Color in the carousel horse using lots of bright colors.

Put a tick by them if you found these things in the park:

Wollman Rink
Balto, the sled dog
Carousel
Bethesda Fountain
A lake
A bridge
Hans Christian Andersen
Alice in Wonderland
Strawberry Fields
Belvedere Castle

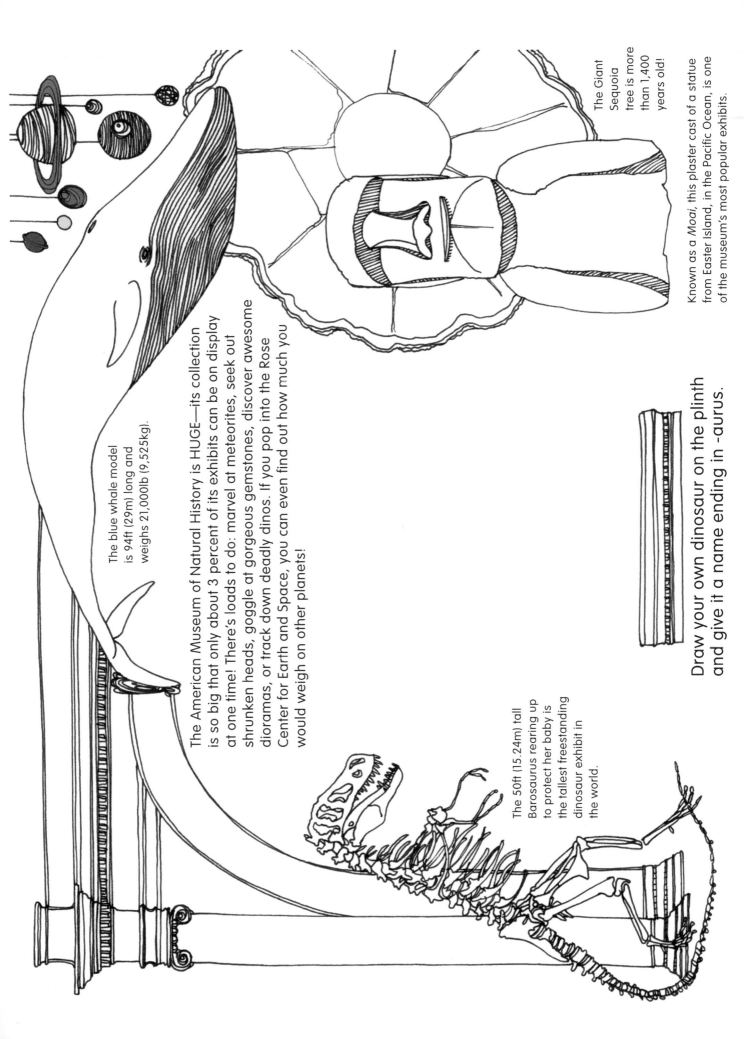

The Giant Sequoia tree is more than 1,400 years old!

Known as a *Moai*, this plaster cast of a statue from Easter Island, in the Pacific Ocean, is one of the museum's most popular exhibits.

The blue whale model is 94ft (29m) long and weighs 21,000lb (9,525kg).

The American Museum of Natural History is HUGE—its collection is so big that only about 3 percent of its exhibits can be on display at one time! There's loads to do: marvel at meteorites, seek out shrunken heads, goggle at gorgeous gemstones, discover awesome dioramas, or track down deadly dinos. If you pop into the Rose Center for Earth and Space, you can even find out how much you would weigh on other planets!

The 50ft (15.24m) tall Barosaurus rearing up to protect her baby is the tallest freestanding dinosaur exhibit in the world.

Draw your own dinosaur on the plinth and give it a name ending in -aurus.

Draw a picture of another interesting thing you saw at the museum.
What was the best thing you saw in the museum?

Design your own sports shirt.

Join the dots to complete the basketball player.

Can you spot the 5 differences between the hockey players?

Madison Square Garden is a huge multipurpose indoor stadium that stages lots of events including concerts, parties, hockey, wrestling, basketball, and dog shows. It's also home to the New York Knicks basketball team and the New York Rangers hockey team.

If you could go to any event at Madison Square Garden, what would it be? Draw a picture of it.

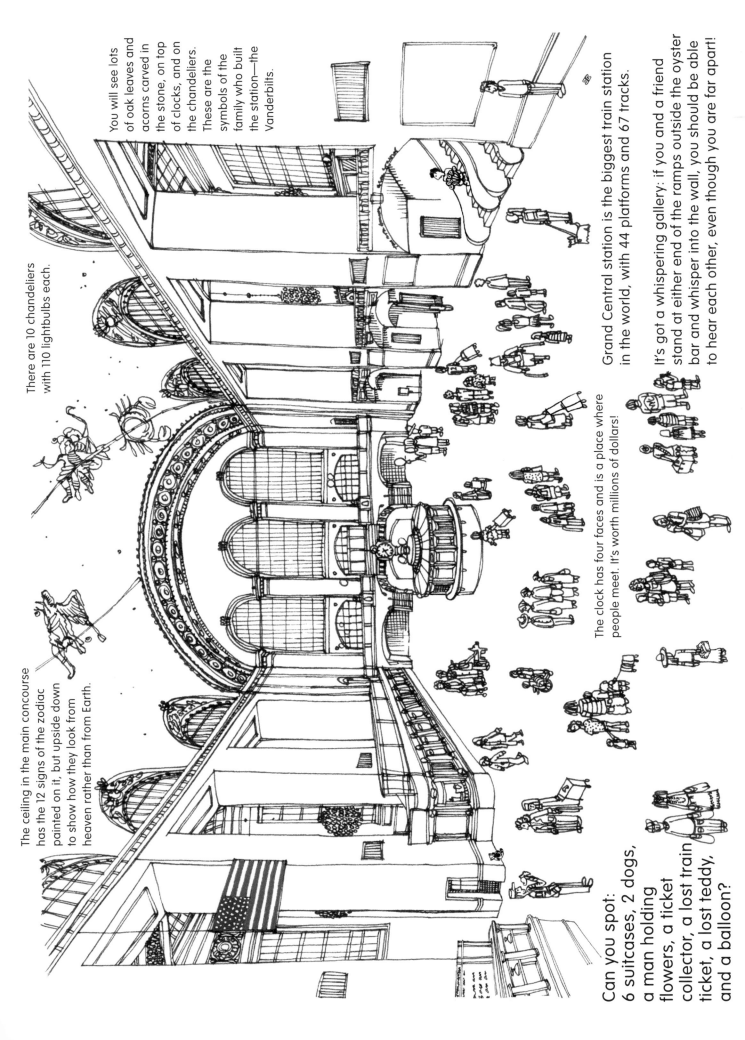

There are 10 chandeliers with 110 lightbulbs each.

The ceiling in the main concourse has the 12 signs of the zodiac painted on it, but upside down to show how they look from heaven rather than from Earth.

You will see lots of oak leaves and acorns carved in the stone, on top of clocks, and on the chandeliers. These are the symbols of the family who built the station—the Vanderbilts.

Grand Central station is the biggest train station in the world, with 44 platforms and 67 tracks.

It's got a whispering gallery: if you and a friend stand at either end of the ramps outside the oyster bar and whisper into the wall, you should be able to hear each other, even though you are far apart!

The clock has four faces and is a place where people meet. It's worth millions of dollars!

Can you spot:
6 suitcases, 2 dogs, a man holding flowers, a ticket collector, a lost train ticket, a lost teddy, and a balloon?

Draw a picture of the clock. You won't be able to show all four faces, though!

Color me in … Cut me out … Dress me up!

Hotel doorman

Firefighter

Upper East Side lady

Police officer

Draw other uniforms you have seen people wear in New York. Use another piece of paper if you need to. You could draw a chef with a hat and apron, a baseball player, or even a department store Santa.

The Statue of Liberty was a gift from France to America in 1886. She is made from iron and covered in copper, which has turned green as she has aged. Visitors have to climb 377 stairs to reach her crown, where there are 25 windows to look out of. Other famous sights you will see from the East River include the Staten Island Ferry and the Manhattan skyline with its massive skyscrapers.

Join the dots to complete the picture of the Statue of Liberty. Then color it in green.

Can you join the dots on the skyscrapers without taking your pen off the page?

Did you know, the Statue of Liberty wears a size 879 shoe?

Staten Island Ferry

Draw a new outfit for the Statue of Liberty to wear.

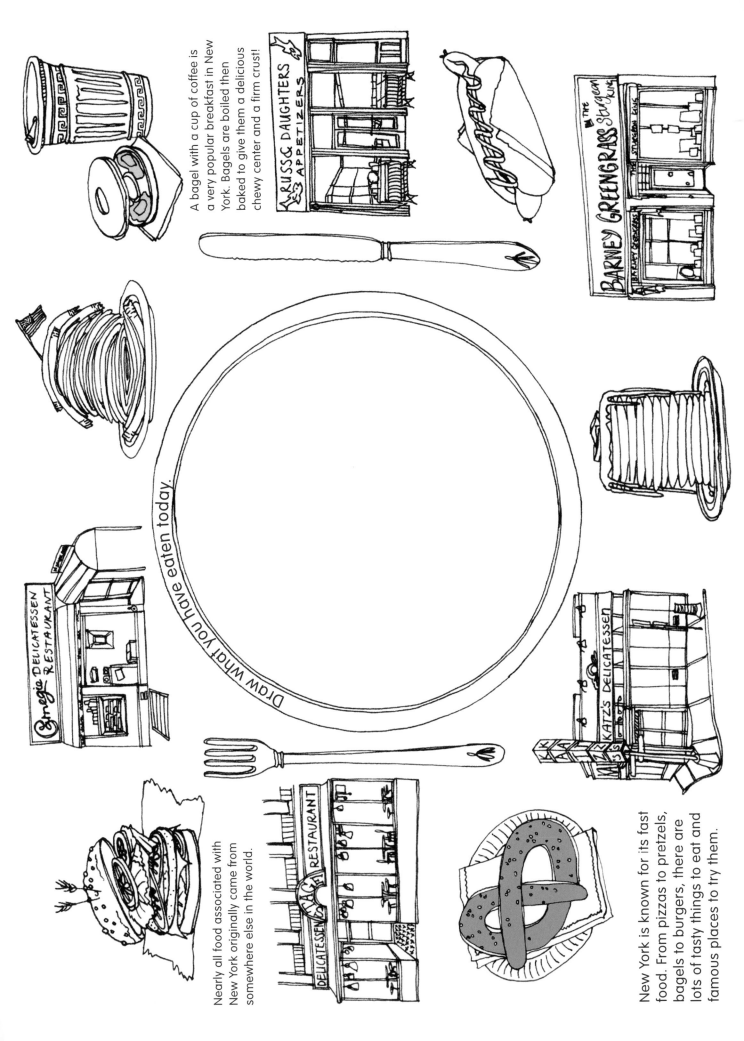

A bagel with a cup of coffee is a very popular breakfast in New York. Bagels are boiled then baked to give them a delicious chewy center and a firm crust!

Draw what you have eaten today.

Nearly all food associated with New York originally came from somewhere else in the world.

New York is known for its fast food. From pizzas to pretzels, bagels to burgers, there are lots of tasty things to eat and famous places to try them.

There are lots of themed restaurants in New York, ranging from the Wild West to Hollywood movie sets, with singing waitstaff and people performing theater or magic tricks. Draw a restaurant and give it a theme. Then draw the food you would sell there.

Times Square has lots of billboards advertising the latest cool thing to buy. Fill in the blank billboards with your own adverts. How about designing an advert for sunglasses, snacks, or a toy?

This huge intersection of Broadway and Seventh Avenue, known as Times Square, is the number 1 tourist spot in the USA. There are lots of big stores, great places to eat, and the world's largest TV screen.

By law every building must have an illuminated sign on its front, so Times Square is a vast sea of flashing neon.

M&M's World has a 17ft (5m) Statue of Liberty made out of green M&M's!

Hundreds of thousands of people gather in Times Square to see in the New Year, when a giant shiny ball slides down a pole on the stroke of midnight.

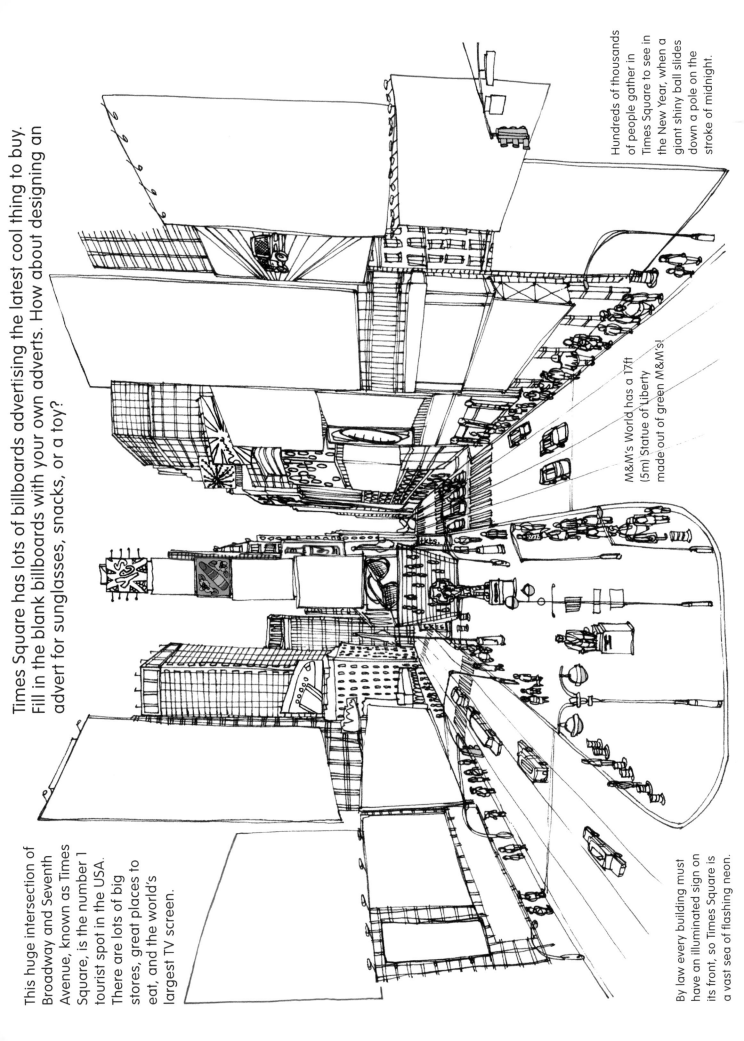

Draw a picture of one of the costumed characters you've seen in Times Square.

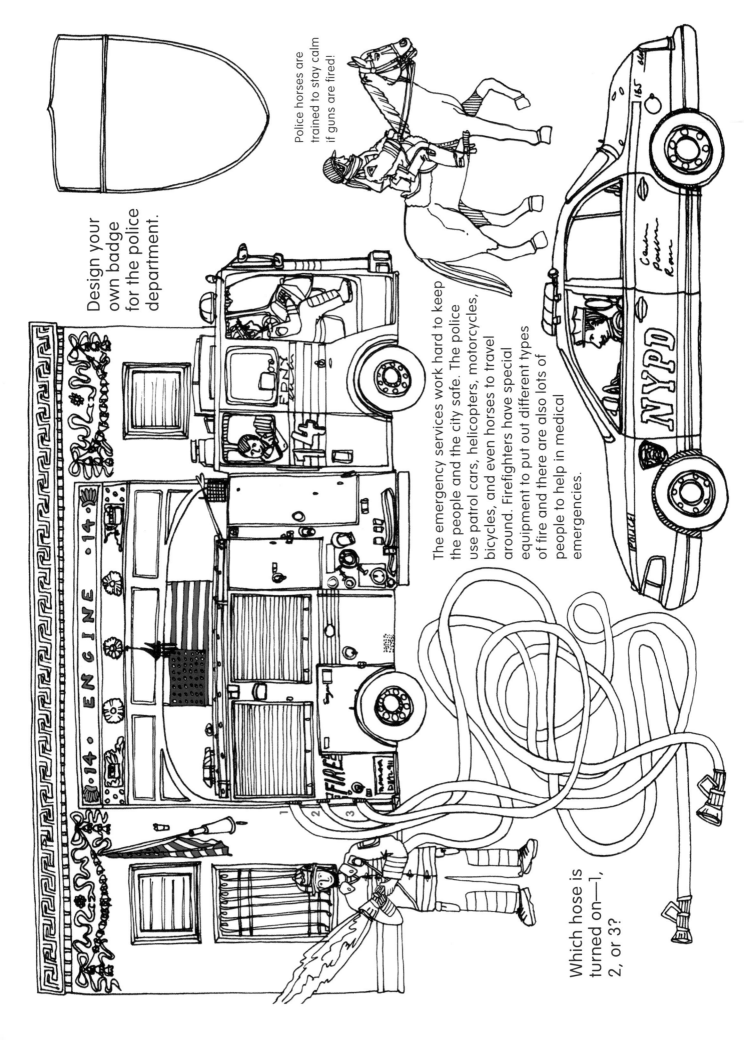

Design your own badge for the police department.

Police horses are trained to stay calm if guns are fired!

The emergency services work hard to keep the people and the city safe. The police use patrol cars, helicopters, motorcycles, bicycles, and even horses to travel around. Firefighters have special equipment to put out different types of fire and there are also lots of people to help in medical emergencies.

Which hose is turned on—1, 2, or 3?

ENGINE ·14·

NYPD

Design another badge, this time for the fire department.

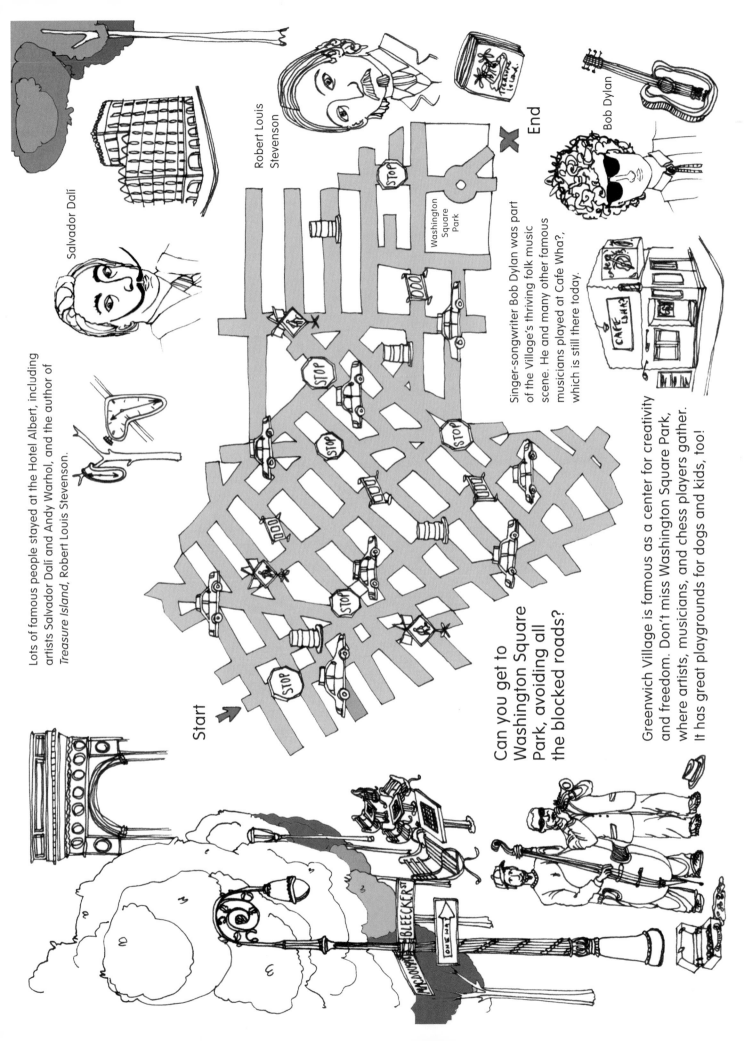

Lots of famous people stayed at the Hotel Albert, including artists Salvador Dali and Andy Warhol, and the author of *Treasure Island*, Robert Louis Stevenson.

Salvador Dali

Robert Louis Stevenson

Bob Dylan

Singer-songwriter Bob Dylan was part of the Village's thriving folk music scene. He and many other famous musicians played at Cafe Wha?, which is still there today.

Greenwich Village is famous as a center for creativity and freedom. Don't miss Washington Square Park, where artists, musicians, and chess players gather. It has great playgrounds for dogs and kids, too!

Can you get to Washington Square Park, avoiding all the blocked roads?

Start

End

Washington Square Park

STOP

BLEECKER ST

ONE WAY

Every year, Greenwich Village hosts the biggest Halloween parade in the world, with spectacular giant puppets and eye-catching costumes. It's watched by more than 2 million people! Design a scary mask for Halloween.

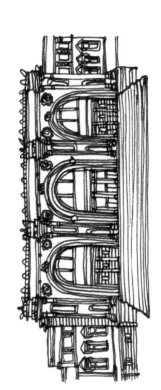

New York is full of wonderful art galleries and museums to visit. Inside you will find everything from ancient artifacts, sculptures, and famous paintings to dinosaur skeletons and mummies.

The Starry Night by Vincent Van Gogh, Museum of Modern Art

Boating by Édouard Manet, Metropolitan Museum of Art

Paint, draw, or doodle your own work of art.

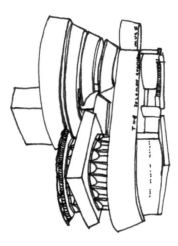

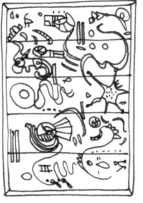

Striped by Vasily Kandinsky, Guggenheim Museum

Alligator Skull by Earl Staley, New Museum

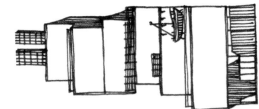

Look in a mirror and draw a self-portrait.